IRISH
ILLUMINATED
MANUSCRIPTS

IRISH ILLUMINATED MANUSCRIPTS

of the Early Christian Period

INTRODUCTION BY

JAMES JOHNSON SWEENEY

A MENTOR-UNESCO ART BOOK

PUBLISHED BY
THE NEW AMERICAN LIBRARY, INC.
BY ARRANGEMENT WITH UNESCO

FIRST PRINTING, DECEMBER, 1965

MENTOR TRADEMARK REG. U. S. PAT. OFF. AND FOREIGN COUNTRIES
REGISTERED TRADEMARK—MARCA REGISTRADA

MENTOR-UNESCO ART BOOKS ARE PUBLISHED BY
THE NEW AMERICAN LIBRARY, INC.
1301 AVENUE OF THE AMERICAS, NEW YORK, NEW YORK 10019

PRINTED IN ITALY BY AMILCARE PIZZI S.P.A., MILANO

Of the wealth of Irish manuscripts which has come down to us from the early centuries of the Christian era, two in particular, the *Book of Durrow* and the *Book of Kells*, stand as monuments of artistic achievement in that critical period in the history of West European culture. The former dates from the dawn of that rich flowering of Christian art in Ireland, the influence of which was to spread so far into continental Europe during the next two centuries; the latter, from the time at which this art had attained its fullest and most idiosyncratic development. Neither was completely cut off from what had gone before, nor from what was to follow. Still, no work of parallel quality in similar character to the former has come down to us. Both are distinctly different from the Ottonian, the Carolingian and High Renaissance styles which stand historically between them and us. And, paradoxically enough, it is just the features which distinguish those two gospel-books from illuminated manuscripts nearer in time to our period that bring them closest to the live art of the present century.

Today we find that the intensity, imagination and freedom with which the script in both these books is handled, the sharp, clear outlines of the illuminations and the epigrammatic concision of image are what particularly appeal to our taste. The characteristics which writers schooled to a nineteenth-century view criticized most sharply offer us little difficulty today—little that is aesthetically unfamiliar. For example, as O. Elfrida Saunders says in *English Illumination*, " There is no attempt at representation of solidity and the colour is quite

5

arbitrary. Hair may be painted blue or even different colours in stripes.... An effect of broken colour is aimed at, even in figure representations: the clothes form either a harlequin pattern of patches or stripes of different colours.... In these manuscripts, the same awkwardnesses due to an entire ignorance of perspective are seen as in early Egyptian tomb-paintings; a body is represented in full view while the sides and feet are shown; or a side view of the nose is placed on a face which is turned frontwards."

Our present-day hospitality to such a free handling of compositional elements in the visual arts is the fruit of a struggle carried on during the past five decades by artists who realized the importance of breaking from the strait-jacket of representational conventions inherited from the classical and Renaissance worlds, and the possibilities of expression such a liberation would open up. The Irish artists of the *Book of Durrow*, the *Book of Kells* and other related manuscripts came to this freedom of outlook naturally. It was part of their heritage. They had no strait-jacket out of which they had to break. At the western extremity of Europe, they had few links with classical Greece or Rome. Their art was a natural growth by assimilation. We recognize in the spiral designs and " trumpet patterns ", so characteristic of it, the influence of their Celtic metal-working forbears. We see in the interlace, the fret and the ecclesiastical iconography, evidence of an acquaintanceship with Syrian and Coptic manuscripts, either brought to Ireland by the missionaries or seen by the scribes abroad. Later, in the interlaced animal motifs, we have an unquestionable response on the part of the Irish illuminators to the same features in Germanic or Celtic decoration—different as they become in their Irish adaptation from both these apparent sources. Basic to all this, and indeed the essential discipline of the Irish illuminator's art, is their scrupulous and individual script which they clearly regarded as an aesthetic expression in itself, not merely as a utilitarian vehicle.

" In no other part of Europe and at no other period of European art ", as Professor A. A. Luce has written in the preface to the Urs Graf-Verlag facsimile edition of the *Book of Durrow*, " has script been treated with greater intensity, imagination, and freedom than in insular book illustration from the seventh to the ninth century. Here alone a level of perfection is reached that can be compared with Islamic or Chinese calligraphy; judged by this standard all pre-Carolingian continental calligraphy looks poor and clumsy."

" The significance of the Irish script as a cultural symptom ", Professor Ludwig Bieler writes in *Ireland, Harbinger of the Middle Ages*, " emerges most clearly when its genesis is compared with that of other 'national scripts' of the early Middle Ages. All the others—the Visigothic script in Spain, the Beneventan script in southern Italy, the local types of the Merovingian kingdom, the Rhaetian and Alemmanic scripts in the districts of Chur and St. Gall, and the less characteristic scripts of northern Italy and western Germany—can be understood as attempts at normalizing the degenerate cursive script of late antiquity in the hope of thus producing a serviceable book-hand. The Irish script, it seems, was a deliberate creation out of elements of several scripts inherited from antiquity which the earliest missionaries had brought with them."

Professor Luce points out the fusion which the scribes achieved in the assimilation of their heritage and their borrowings: " The script element taken over from the ancient world is integrated in an ornamental style that had been developed to a high point by the Celts of the Iron Age." And he stresses the fact that this ornamentation was an art in its own right and not, like later ornament, a mere accessory to figurative representation.

This is the essential individuality of Irish illumination throughout its great period: the complete integration of every factor in the book, in spite of a jealous discreteness in each detail, given its character by discipline of the script.

Even before the *Book of Durrow*, we have an austere exemplification of this in the *Cathach* of Saint Columba. This is a preciously conceived book, the earliest surviving manuscript in Irish majuscule (in all probability, from the end of the sixth century); it boasts little ornament beyond

simple hollow initials ending in small spirals and surrounded, in certain instances, by lines of dots which
introduce each psalm. According to the palaeographer
Lowe, the *Cathach* " represents the pure milk of Irish
calligraphy ". And, while it is generally conceded to be the
earliest specimen of national script in Ireland, it already
announces in its integrity, its clarity and the concreteness
of its detail, the great works (more colourful if no less
intense) to come after it (see page 9).

Today the clarity, intensity and definition of these
masterworks of Irish illumination (and of others such as
the *Book of Armagh*, the *Stowe Missal*, and the *Book of
the Dun Cow*) may come as a surprise to those who
associate the term " Celtic " with the vague, the misty
and the mystical, as the result of a concept which had its
roots in the beginnings of the Romantic revival in the mid-
eighteenth century and its exhaustion in the " Celtic
twilight " movement of the 1890s. It was Thomas Gray
who invented the Bard; and, as Robin Flower stated in his
Sir John Rhŷs Memorial Lecture, *Ireland and Mediaeval
Europe*, " There could be nothing less like the poeṭ of the
Irish or of the Welsh Middle Ages than the mystic suicide
of this famous ode." Macpherson's *Ossian* filled in the
details; and since Macpherson's time " vagueness and mist
and an indefinite use of dubiously poetic language has been
generally held to be the indubitable mask of Celticism."

Actually the truth is the extreme antithesis of this.
Flower adds, " I think if I were asked what characteristic
was to be found everywhere in Irish literature from the
first records down to the tales and popular sayings among
the peasantry today, the answer must necessarily be: a
sharp and homely brevity of epigrammatic speech ...[*] the
concrete cast of language ... the pleasure in sharp bright
colour. ..." And in a footnote to a published lecture he
quotes a statement by H. Idris Bell on the poetry of the
mediaeval Welsh poets, the " Gogynfeirdd ", towards the
end of the eleventh century, and on early Welsh poetry in
general: " Even further from the truth is the idea that
Celtic poetry is misty and loves subdued colours. On the
contrary, its characteristic is sharp, clear outline, a cloud-

The Cathach. *End of sixth century. Dublin, Royal Irish Academy.
23.5 x 15.5 cm. Surviving fragment of folio 21r.*

9

less atmosphere, a passion for bright primary colours."
This, Flower comments, " is true, *mutatis mutandis,* of
Irish poetry also."

And, *mutatis mutandis,* as we may see from the *Book
of Durrow* and the *Book of Kells,* of mediaeval Irish
illumination.

The *Book of Durrow* is a gospel manuscript named after
the monastery of Durrow, a foundation of Saint Columba
near Tullamore in central Ireland. Here it was kept from
the eleventh century (if not before) until the seventeenth
century, when, after the dissolution of the monastery—as
we know from an entry in the *Martyrology of Donegal* and
from a mention in Conall MacGeoghegan's translations
(1627) of the *Annals of Clonmacnoise*—it passed to one of
the MacGeoghegans, who would soak it in water which
was then used as a cure for sick cattle. In 1661 it came
into the possession of Henry Jones, a Cromwellian army
scout master who had become the Protestant Bishop of
Meath and Vice-Chancellor of Trinity College, Dublin.
Eventually Jones gave it to Trinity College, in whose library
it is still kept.

Monasticism had been introduced into Ireland in the
fifth century. The *Book of Armagh* reports that Saint
Patrick used to distribute books of law and books of the
gospel to his newly founded monasteries; and it was no
doubt not long before the copying and decorating of books
became a regular part of the work of the monks. Saint
Columba, also known in Irish as Colum-Cille, " the Dove
of the Churches ", founded a number of monasteries in the
sixth century, including Durrow and Derry. According to
tradition, Columba was himself an ardent copyist and is
reported to have written 300 manuscripts in his own hand.
Indeed, legend reports that it was a dispute over the
possession of a manuscript which led to his self-exile to
Iona in 565.

Whatever the truth of the story, Columba's exile was
fruitful for English art as well as for English Christianity,
for it led to the introduction of Celtic manuscript painting
into the north of Britain. Seventy years later, in 635, Irish

monks from Iona under Aidan set forth into Northumbria and founded the monastery of Lindisfarne, which soon became famous under Saint Cuthbert (ob. 687). And the *Lindisfarne Gospels* (British Museum MS Cotton Nero D. IV), that magnificent surviving example of those monks' work at the end of the seventh or beginning of the eighth century, shows that they were little behind their Irish contemporaries in the art of illumination.

Bede reports that in the latter part of the seventh century many Angles went to Ireland for a time to study, so that by the end of that century there were no doubt in Britain a number of monastic artists who were trained to carry on the work of the Irish illuminators, as well as actual Irish manuscripts to serve them as models.

The *Book of Durrow* is a small manuscript (24 x 16.5 cm.) and an early one, though its date is difficult to fix with any certainty. It is generally regarded as having been written toward the close of the seventh century. Gwynn thought it not later than A.D. 650, Lindsay about 700. Bruce-Mitford places it in the neighbourhood of 680-85, on the assumption that the *Lindisfarne Gospels* were completed about 698 and granting the direct affiliation between the monasteries of Lindisfarne in Northumbria and Durrow in Meath. However, as Professor Luce points out, the *Book of Durrow* might be the product of another scriptorium which continued an earlier style, and then its date could be independent of Lindisfarne for, as he writes, " many manuscripts of high quality must have been lost. One should be careful not to postulate too close a connexion between those manuscripts which have happened to survive."

In any case, the *Book of Durrow* is clearly earlier than the gospels of Saint Willibrord from Echternach (*Codex Epternacensis*, Paris Bib. Nat. Lat. 9389), attributed by Zimmermann to the middle of the eighth century. In it there is no bird theme on any of the seven " carpet " pages and the animal theme occurs but once (Plate 7). Zoomorphic ornament is used only to a very limited extent and is not associated with the decoration of the script. Throughout it preserves a primitive, pristine character. The text (monograms and decorated capitals) carries a developed Celtic curvilinear ornament of hair-spring coil and small trumpet type. Such ornament can be seen to have evolved directly from the script embellishments of the early *Cathach* of Saint Columba, thus establishing a relationship in time subsequent to that work. But for all its primitiveness one factor which holds it on the seventh-century horizon is indicated by Nils Åberg, namely that "during the seventh century, mainland Germanic art [first] took firm root in Anglo-Saxon England". From it is derived this single example in the *Book of Durrow* (Plate 7) while the rest of the book is Celtic in style.

Professor Ludwig Bieler in his introduction to the Urs Graf-Verlag facsimile edition of the *Book of Durrow* places the book halfway between the Durham manuscript fragment and the *Codex Epternacensis,* both manuscripts of Northumbrian origin.

Finally, Professor Luce proposes a date of A.D. 630.

Just as the dating of the *Book of Durrow* is difficult to fix with any precision, so the place of origin of this codex also remains debatable. T. K. Abbott in 1895 believed he had established that the text had its roots in Northumbria. Zimmermann felt convinced that the artist of the *Codex Epternacensis,* executed in Northumbria, had been influenced by the *Book of Durrow.* And Ludwig Bieler explains that " if palaeographers are inclined to place the *Book of Durrow* in Northumbria it is because it fits better into the known development of Irish script in that kingdom, whereas in our present state of knowledge it would be rather a stranger among manuscripts known to have been written in Ireland."

On the other side of the question Professor Luce writes, in his preface to the facsimile edition, " I have not stated that the *Book of Durrow* was written in Ireland ... but neither have I left its provenance an entirely open question on which anyone may think as he pleases. The final word about it has yet to be said, and that word cannot be said until the world of art and letters has had time to consider its history, its historical setting and its kinship with other documents of the Columban *parochia.* Meantime, in view of prevailing trends, largely due to the partial views and

12

sheer mistakes, I ought to add that the *prima facie* probabilities are so strongly in favour of the Irish origin of the codex that the *onus probandi* lies fairly and squarely on the shoulders of those who think it of English origin."

The fact remains that no matter where its geographical source may have been, whether Durrow or Northumbria, it was essentially a product of that school of manuscript illumination which the Irish followers of Columba had fostered, a school rooted in the tradition of late La Tène ornament, a firmly established style of decorative art in which the new demands made by the Christian Church were able to find a place.

Early as the *Book of Durrow* may be, we see in it the artistic type of the Irish gospel-book already fully developed. Each gospel is preceded by the symbol of the Evangelist enclosed in a border or ornamental frame (Plates 2 to 4), by a page of rich ornament (Plate 1) and, as an opening of the text, by an initial in a matching style (Plate 6).

At the beginning of the book are found a few ornamental pages based on the form of the cross, another page with symbols of the Evangelists in the corners of the cross and the Eusebian Canon Tables (lists of parallel passages in the various gospels in ornamental frames or archways). At the end there is a page with a pattern of squares (folio 248r). In addition to the opening passages of the four gospels there are ornamental initials in two other places: they elaborate the Chi-Rho " autem generatio " after the Genealogy of Christ in Saint Matthew, and the " fuit in diebus Herodis " after the prologue of Saint Luke (Plate 6). Ornamental initials on a smaller scale occur here and there in the prefatory matter. The entire ornamentation of the codex is planned in every detail. The same plan, though more developed, underlies the ornamentation of the *Lindisfarne Gospels* and the *Book of Kells*. In fact, this plan set the fashion not only for these two later works but also for many other gospel-books in Northumbria and on the Continent. And, as Ludwig Bieler has written, it is evident that such a well-designed plan as this " must have originated either in the mind of an individual or within a closely knit spiritual community. In any event it

13

must have been the product of a very definite spiritual and artistic milieu. One cannot help thinking in this connexion of that great community of Irish monks, the familia Colum-Cille."

Within this plan the "vocabulary" of ornamental motifs in the *Book of Durrow* draws on sources of widely different origin. There are the inherited spirals and "trumpets" of the La Tène Celtic art (Plate 1) which, like the millefiori and cloisonné, were translated from metal and enamel to the book page. As early as the *Cathach*, as we have mentioned above, the dot-edging is already found. In the *Book of Durrow*, these rows of dots are not only around the contours of letters, as in Plate 6, but also in places are superimposed on the interlacing ribbon (Plate 5). Scattered in small groups, preferably groups of three for symbolic associations, they also serve the purpose of filling empty spaces.

The most striking ornamental feature of the *Book of Durrow* is, however, the broad band interlacing, framed by double lines (Plates 3 and 4), which has its counterpart in stone on the slightly later crosses of Fahan Mura and Carndonagh in County Donegal; and later still, on the two older side plates of the silver book shrine, the Domnach Airgid, in the National Museum, Dublin. This broad band interlacing soon gave way to a narrow thread or string variety. Actually, interlacing of one kind or another is found in mediaeval art over a wide area. It seems, however, to be significant that the band interlacing as a frame of the written page, as we have it around the illustrations in the *Book of Durrow*, occurs first in the Syriac *Gospels of Rabula* (now in the Laurentian Library, Florence) and later in Coptic manuscripts of the eighth and ninth centuries. Another link with Coptic and Syriac art is the predominant colour scheme of red, green and yellow in the illumination of the *Book of Durrow*, where the artist sets these colours off by the use of a deep black for the background and for the filling of blanks.

Special note should be given to folio 192v (Plate 7) which faces the opening page of Saint John, a unique page in this codex. Here a circular medallion, which forms the centre of the composition, is surrounded by friezes of animal interlacing. As Ludwig Bieler points out, the centrepiece has a close Coptic parallel and a long iconographic pedigree, and has been plausibly explained by Victor H. Elbern as a Trinitarian symbol. "The animal interlacing, on the other hand," writes Bieler, " is the first appearance in Irish illumination of a characteristic motif of Teutonic art. But even here, at its first occurrence in an Irish manuscript, the motif is treated with a difference. Not only is the individual animal more isolated, not to say independent, and less twisted than is common in Germanic art; it also retains more of its anatomy, as is exemplified by the comparatively naturalistic treatment of the legs. The difference becomes evident to anyone who compares the page from the *Book of Durrow* with animal interlacing from Scandinavia, for example, or metal from the Sutton Hoo Find in the British Museum. This greater vitality in ornamental animals remains characteristic of Irish art for a long time, both in metal and on the vellum page: its animal bodies, however drawn out, sinuous and contorted they may be, at least always have heads and extremities that give some impression of realism. Among the smaller drawings in the *Book of Kells* where the principle of abstraction was not so strictly adhered to, we find in the work of one particular illuminator most appealing representations of animals—hound and hare, fish and otter, and many others—in a quite realistic style."

" But though the connexion is certain, northern interlacings have an unmistakeable quality of their own," Peter Meyer points out in his " Notes on the Art and Ornament " in the facsimile edition. " There is not one Coptic interlacing that could be mistaken for a northern interlacing, and vice versa; and it is well known that this style persisted in Scandinavia well into the thirteenth century, while the Continent as a whole reverted to the Roman-Hellenistic and Byzantine-Hellenistic traditions at the time of the Carolingian Renaissance. Both in Coptic and in Lombardic versions of interlacing, emphasis is placed on intelligible forms such as circles, oblongs, crosses, etc., and the interlacing never quite abandons its role as a mere frame—a role that dates back to the Roman pavements. Northern interlacing, on the other hand, is autonomous. It avoids of set purpose the creation of intelligible geometrical forms and is bound up with spiral and animal ornaments alien to southern interlacing. It is far more abstract and intricate; much more imagination and care is expended on it; the execution is much more precise."

A link between script and illumination is established by ornamental initials. Unlike the early continental scribes who, regardless of context, put an enlarged capital at the beginning of a page or even a column, the Irish scribe and illuminator, however keen he may be on decorating his manuscript, does not for a moment forget that the initial is part of the text and should be used as a means to its articulation. This idea, as Bieler states, "already dominates the ornamentation of the *Cathach*; each psalm begins with an initial; the letters immediately following are not written in the ordinary text hand, but form a transition, in both size and elaboration, from one to the other. The same is done for the *Book of Durrow* and in other illuminated manuscripts of the Irish and Anglo-Saxon schools, only in a more elaborate and sophisticated form." In the *Book of Durrow*, for example, the large initial which grows in size and richness of ornament from one gospel to another is regularly followed by a smaller initial of the same style, which in turn is continued by one or more lines of ornamental script framed by a hollow band, or dotted oblong (Plate 6). In the *Book of Durrow* these letters are normally hollow, filled in with colour or black and always, by various devices, united into one artistic unit.

The greatest achievement in Irish manuscript illumination, the *Book of Kells*, was formerly held to be earlier than the *Lindisfarne Gospels* (which are dated approximately from A.D. 700) but is now generally assigned to the late eighth or early ninth century. It can only have been made in one of two places: Iona or Kells. It seems probable, though, that due to its resemblances to the *Lindisfarne Gospels* it was at least begun at Iona, from which Lindisfarne had been colonized about the year 635.

In 804, after two Viking raids, the monks of Iona fled from their exposed island monastery to Meath, in Ireland. They obtained a grant of land at Cenannus (Kells) and established there the metropolis of the Columban Order. But they regretted abandoning Iona and made various attempts to resettle there, carrying with them the sacred objects and books of the monastery. Finally in 849 all were brought back to Kells, the great manuscript probably with them.

That the manuscript was at Kells two centuries later we know from an entry in the *Annals of Ulster* (A.D. 1007). And as it is hardly probable that such a work should have been begun during the troubled years between 804 and 849 (and since most of its decoration points to a date within the eighth century) it is reasonable to assume that an important part of it had been produced in the scriptorium of Iona before the Viking raids drove the monks to Meath.

There is a possibility that all the work was done in Iona and that the unfinished state of the manuscript is due to the destruction of the monastery by the Vikings and the subsequent flight to Kells. But it may also be that only part of the decoration had been completed at the time of the exodus and that the fugitive monks continued their work in the new monastery.

In any case the most probable date of the *Book of Kells* is between 760-804 and 815-20; and it is likely that different painters were working at it for several years. Again, in view of A. M. Friend's evidence that in its Canon Tables and Evangelist portraits it has borrowed motifs from the continental Ada Group, these elements must be dated at the earliest about the close of the eighth century.

The *Book of Kells* is a manuscript of the gospels of rather large size (33 x 24 cm.), written on thick glazed vellum. Its pages were originally still larger; but a binder, a century or so ago, clipped away their margins, cutting even into the edges of the illuminations. Five leaves are missing, and also the portrait of the Evangelist Saint John; but they seem to have been lost for centuries. Otherwise the manuscript is in relatively good condition, in spite of another earlier misadventure. The story of this is well known from the account in the *Annals of Ulster*: " the great gospel of Colum-Cille, the chief relic of the Western world, on account of its wrought shrine ", was " wickedly stolen in the night from the western sacristy of the great stone church of Cenannus " and was found a few months later stripped of its gold, under a sod.

After the surrender of the monastery of Kells to the Crown by Abbot Richard Plunket in 1539, the manuscript passed into the hands of one Geralde Plunket of Dublin, possibly a relative of the abbot, and from Plunket to James Ussher, a highly versatile and accomplished scholar of the day, and one of the earliest students of Trinity College, Dublin. Finally the manuscript passed with Ussher's library to Trinity College, where it is today.

The *Book of Kells* did not perhaps owe the high esteem in which it was held by its possessors in the eleventh century altogether to the exquisite beauty of its penmanship. Such manuscripts were then doubtless more numerous in Ireland and excited less wonder and admiration then than now. The antiquity of the volume, and its being regarded as the autograph of Colum-Cille or at least as having been in his possession, are much more likely causes of the veneration accorded to it.

At the beginning of the eleventh century the book belonged to the church of Kells and was called " the great gospel of Colum-Cille ", either because Colum-Cille was supposed to have written it, or because it belonged to one of the principal monastic establishments of his Order in Ireland. When it is said that the *Book of Kells* may have been written by Columba it is not meant that he was also the artist from whose pen the elaborate ornamentation of the volume proceeded. Columba was reputed to have been a most industrious, indeed almost fanatical, scribe. But the scribe and the illuminator were seldom the same person. The illuminations were frequently executed much later than the manuscript itself and the original plan of the *Book of Kells* was apparently so vast that it could not be completed in a short time. The spaces to be decorated were left blank by the scribe. Several painters, possibly at different periods, were employed to fill them; there are, indeed, still to be seen some pages where the ornaments of the framework are unfinished, being only partially sketched in outline.

The script employed in the *Book of Kells* is the beautiful round uncial of all the best Irish manuscripts. It differs little in that feature from the *Book of Durrow*. But here their similarities cease. The scale of the *Book of Kells* is different from that of the *Book of Durrow,* and the mood of its expression is vastly different: the calm, meticulous distinction of the earlier book gives way to a flamboyant, magnificent exuberance; there is nothing of that constrained perfection of order and organization which mark both the *Book of Durrow* and the *Lindisfarne Gospels,* inherited from the *Cathach* of Saint Columba.

No manuscript we have seen before approaches the *Book of Kells* for elaborate ornamentation. The cover pages have a cruciform composition, followed by a series of porticos framing the Canon Tables. Each gospel begins with a portrait of its author or of some other introductory figure and a page where the enlarged letters of the first words nearly disappear under the decoration. The carpet pages of pure ornament of the *Book of Durrow* are replaced in the *Book of Kells* by cruciform pages bearing the symbols of the Evangelists and the same symbols, disposed in various ways over and under the arcades, give the Canon Tables a fantastic appearance. The Chi-Rho introducing the Genealogy of Christ in Saint Matthew is ornamented as richly as the initial pages of the gospels.

A continuous chain of ornamentation runs through the text. The capitals at the beginning of each paragraph— two, three, four to a page—are made of brightly coloured entwinements of birds, snakes, distorted men and quadrupeds, fighting or performing all sorts of acrobatic feats. Other animals wander about the pages between the lines or on top of them.

One of the most striking and unusual features of the *Book of Kells* is this profusion of animated capitals, a feature of Irish illumination which may owe its origin to the ornamented letters ending in coiled spirals in the *Book of Durrow.*

Oriental and particularly Coptic influence is generally recognized throughout the *Book of Kells*—Coptic clearly in

The Book of Armagh. A.D. *807-808. Dublin, Trinity College Library.*
20 x 15 cm. Symbols of the Four Evangelists (folio 32r).

the group of red dots on the robes of the Evangelists Mark and John. Furthermore, the figure of the Virgin and Child seated on a throne surrounded by attending angels appears frequently in Coptic art. Françoise Henry points out a striking analogy between the famous page reproduced in Plate 9 and a ninth-century Coptic manuscript in the Pierpont Morgan Library in New York (*Catalogue of the Manuscripts of the Pierpont Morgan Collection*, Plate 1). It is true that the Coptic manuscripts are all, so far as is known, later than the Irish. But Coptic manuscripts of the ninth to the fourteenth centuries were evidently based on a well-established ancient tradition originating in the sixth (possibly even the fifth) century. This assumption is supported by an early Coptic binding with a decorative arrangement of broad ribbons and crosses which suggest the existence in the sixth century A.D. of full pages of ribbon interlacing. The later Coptic manuscripts which we know probably embody many archaic elements. But it would appear that there must have been a direct connexion between early Irish Christianity and the monasteries of Egypt, as well as the highly orientalized Greek Christianity of the south-east Mediterranean.

Françoise Henry believes that among the several artists who may have worked on the illumination at different periods four are readily identifiable on stylistic grounds. One artist, Miss Henry feels, was obviously entrusted with the cruciform cover page known as " the page of the eight circles " (Plate 16), the great Chi-Rho (Plate 17), and the initial page of each of the gospels, except the Quoniam. She sees in him " the goldsmith ", someone familiar with work in precious metals, in enamel and in niello. The delicacy of his work impresses her, as does his interest in asymmetry. Miss Henry recognizes another individualist in the portraitist of the three Evangelists, the page composed of square frames (Plates 11 and 12), and the Quoniam at the beginning of the Gospel of Saint Luke. The third is the " illustrator ", the author of the *Virgin and Child* (Plate 9), the Tunc Crucifixerat, and the *Temptation* (Plate 23). Finally, a fourth artist is responsible for many less important contributions.

In the lack of constraint which marks the *Book of Kells*, " in the ambiguity and protean gift of metamorphosis of the several elements of a larger composition and generally in the trend towards the ornamental and the abstract, Irish art ", in Ludwig Bieler's view, " reveals a structure of mind " which it would be hard, if not impossible, to describe accurately. But the type of mind which conceived the inexhaustible and extravagant invention of the *Book of Kells* is the same type of mind which in our century gave us James Joyce's *Finnegans Wake*.

It has been said that nothing is more difficult than to form a clear idea of Irish illumination in the eighth and at the beginning of the ninth century, since the number of manuscripts which can be ascribed with certainty to any definite Irish monastery is very small. But one exceptional example has come down to us: the *Book of Armagh*. For although no date is entered in the manuscript the name of the scribe Ferdomnach seems to have been subscribed in at least four places. In the *Annals of Ulster* under the date A.D. 845 appears the obituary record, " Ferdomnach sapiens et scribus optimus Ardamachae ". Ferdomnach is known to have been at Armagh, for a few months only, in 807 and 808.

The *Book of Armagh* is a small volume measuring approximately 20 x 15 x 6 cm. It consisted originally of 222 leaves of vellum. The writing on each side of the leaves is arranged mostly in double columns. It contains copies of documents relating to Saint Patrick (mostly in Latin, but a few are in Irish), the New Testament (Vulgate) —the only copy of the complete New Testament which has been transmitted to our time from the ancient Irish Church—and a " Life of Saint Martin of Tours ".

The illuminations of the *Book of Armagh* are fine pen-drawings which suggest familiarity with enamel work, particularly in the Evangelist symbols (see page 20). The penmanship of the text is of extreme elegance and is admirable throughout for its distinctiveness and uniformity. The character, with a few exceptions, is a miniscule of the type described as " pointed Irish " and is employed for both the Latin and the Irish documents and notes.

Another manuscript which can be dated with some

certainty about the end of the eleventh century and of which part can be reasonably ascribed to a specific artist is the *Lebor na Huidre* (the *Book of the Dun Cow*), MS 23 E25 (Catalogue No. 1229) in the library of the Royal Irish Academy in Dublin, the oldest surviving manuscript entirely in Irish.

Sixty-seven leaves of this book survive, measuring on the average 28 x 20 cm. (a few are smaller). Except for an interpolated page, it is written in two columns in a regular, fairly legible Irish uncial with the beginnings of some sentences in Irish majuscules.

It is felt that there is evidence of the hands of three scribes in the manuscript, though the name with which it is most definitely associated is that of Maelmuire Mac Ceileachair, a member of the Clonmacnoise family of Conn na mBocht, who is known to have died in Clonmacnoise in 1106. For this reason the manuscript is likely to have been written at Clonmacnoise in the last quarter of the eleventh century.

Its name comes from Saint Ciaran's pet cow, whose hide was preserved in the monastery of Clonmacnoise, and is mentioned in several texts as a relic which it was felt brought comfort to a soul departing the body. Its relation to the *Lebor na Huidre* is not clear. Possibly the book had been wrapped in it, or kept in the same building with it; and one tradition holds that the sixth-century original from which this manuscript was copied had been written on the hide itself.

Its decoration consists chiefly of initials which belong to the " wire " and " ribbon " type. In it the oldest surviving version of the *Táin* has been preserved.

As Françoise Henry and Genevieve Marsh-Micheli have written, it represents a transition from the earlier decorated Irish books which are all essentially Latin texts, chiefly gospels and liturgical books, to the decorated books of the fourteenth and fifteenth centuries which are nearly always collections of texts in Irish and never books for ecclesiastical use.

But for all the wealth and variety Irish manuscript illumination has to offer, it is the *Book of Kells* that is generally recognized as the supreme achievement in this field. There is no question but that it is the richest in graphic invention, colour and fantasy. Nevertheless, its overpowering brilliance should not blind us to the quiet distinction, elegant restraint and sensibility of the *Book of Durrow*. Both have their place: one, in a sense, the high point of controlled beauty, almost an artistic understatement; the other a sumptuous, baroque conflagration with, nevertheless, a tight architectural structure. And both share those peculiar characteristics that set them apart from the illuminated work of other cultures and other areas, and which curiously relate them in spirit to the visual approach and the visual appetites of the exploring artists of the present period in the twentieth century—a thousand years and more since the dates of their production.

As Professor Peter Meyer points out, " In the classical conception of art, which again became the rule of the Renaissance, the contents of a picture have a certain independence and mobility with regard to the frame. The frame is to the picture what the window is to the view. Elements within never touch the frame." But in Irish illuminated manuscripts, he continues, " Figures touch figures on different visual planes; the frame attracts figures until they come into contact, or are fitted along it. The position of the figures in the picture of space is thus intentionally confused, the picture and the frame seem to be on the one plane " (Plates 9, 13, 26).

Here we have a natural anticipation of just that objective for which the painters of the late nineteenth and early twentieth century had to fight to win for themselves the integrity of the picture surface—the avoidance of the window-into-space concept of pictorial perspective. Here in the illuminations of the *Book of Kells* one finds that fusion of form and background on a single plane, that unity in a pictorial expression through an avoidance of undue emphases on one or the other which the younger artists were struggling to achieve and on which the younger artists have been building their pictures ever since—even today.

24

ILLUSTRATIONS

1

2

Conall ⁊ ... ...
... ... 1633

Quoniam
quidem mul
ti conati sunt ordinare
narrationem quae
in nobis completae sun
rerum sicut tradiderun
nobis quiabinitio ipsi uiderunt et
ministri fuerunt sermonis uisum est
et mihi adsecuto a principio omni
bus diligenter ex ordine tibi scribe
optime theofile ut cognoscas eorum
uerborum dequib: eruditus es ueritat

FUIT INDIE
bus **HERODIS REGIS**
iudae sacerdos quidam no
mine zacharias de uice abia
et uxor illi de filiabus aaron